CW01333030

The author will surrender to his workshop in a few years. Bottom: bramble of ash. Feather: tuliptree. Beard: sycamore. Body: white and red pear tree. Dress: rosewood. Straps: mahogany. Sock: wenge. Cane: king wood. Top of the hat: white peroba. Glasses: mother-of-pearl. Drops: tin.   60 x 47 cm

Xavier Dyèvre

Best worker of France in marquetry

Translated by Rita Hiraclides

EASY MARQUETRY

An art accessible to everyone   4
What is marquetry ? – Origins

The easiest method "by superposition"   11
Material - Woods - Picture of a swordfish
Use of this method for relatively complicated marquetry   19

Wood veneers   23
Purchase - Fabrication - Types of wood - Particular effects

Marquetry cutting "element by element"   31
Material - Training exercise - Picture of T*he fox and the Stork*
Advice and ideas   50

Frame a marquetry   54
Simple frames - Medallion (musical trophy)

The drawing - Works   58

Complement on woods   62
Classification by color - "Woods of islands" - Straighten and strengthen veneer

Drawings of marquetry   68
Conclusion   79

An art accessible to everyone

*Characteristic marquetry of East of France. Sky: prune tree, walls: magnifying glass, snow: discolored aniegre.
45 x 33cm*

Even without experience with wood work, making marquetry is easy with one normal sleight of hand. When I was animating formations, within five days the trainees could make the fox and the stork picture. The precision varied, but the beauty could be appreciated with hindsight, not in the magnifying glass, what matters is the interest of the drawing and harmony of colors and veins of wood. Marquetry is really easier than say sculptors on wood. My three kids started when they were eight years old, they are fascinated for these divisions of multicolor veneers.

To throw yourself in this beautiful art, you just need a simple table and the least expensive fretsaw sold in DIY stores. Wooden veneers are sent thanks to internet, we use small surfaces.

Previously marquetry artists kept their secrets, but not anymore, fortunately! Thanks to this simple procedure, you will be able to make magnificent paintings in veneers of wood or motives to decorate furniture. You will see that with one book you can learn to make marquetry because everything is easy. If this textbook guides your first steps towards the desire to create, it will have achieved its goal.

What is marquetry?

It's a sort of wooden puzzle of one millimeter of thickness. It completely recovers the support on which it is stuck on; therefore it is not an inlay.

Marquetry, correctly put, represents a drawing, the ancients talked about "wood drawings".

A geometrical assembly of veneers called a wood it will be the subject of the third volume of Easy Marquetry. In the wonderful pallet which offer us "wood of islands" are traditionally added mother-of-pearl, the ivory, the scale of tortoise marinates, the copper, the tin… noble materials of which I speak in the volume 2.

Marquetry can be plated on a simple panel, in the case of a picture or well decorated furniture, a clock, a casket…

"Bonheur du jour" (day happiness) Louis XVI, decorated with tulip wood framed by purpleheart (amaranth) and by nets consisted in box tree and rosewood. The flap carries marquetry of flowers in sycamore, pear tree and lime tree tinged in green, shadowed in the hot sand.

Origins

Prehistoric men inlayed wooden plaques, metals or stones in their utensils and tools to decorate them.

Under the Roman, Greek antiquity and somewhere else on the ground, appeared mosaics on grounds and walls of palaces.

The idea of cutting wooden sheets with a fretsaw to compose real paintings dates the fifteenth century Italy. Other novelty: these puzzles cover their whole support. When done, the laborious diggings of housing in the massive wood.

Italian and German craftsmen came to France to learn their methods in the eighteenth century; the French inlaid furniture reached a beauty that makes the admiration from the whole world.
In the French revolution : end of the corporations of jobs. Under the empire : blockade of precious wooden imports.

A revival in marquetry takes place towards 1905, new art, and 1925, ornamental arts. But the industrialization was right of these interesting attempts.

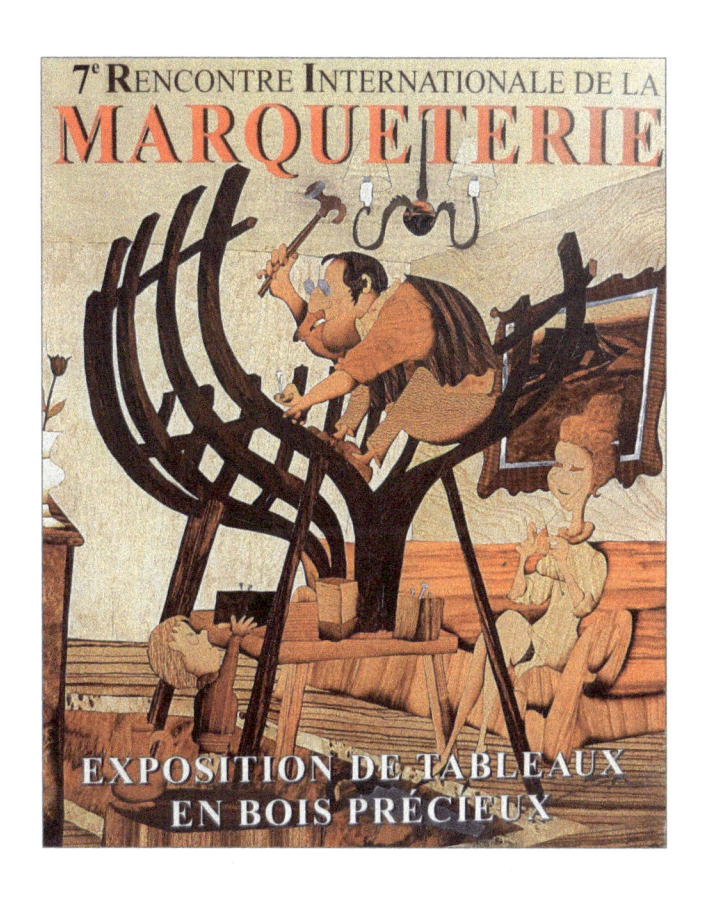

Marquetry from Georges Savery

Musical trophy in a medallion : a characteristic of marquetry in the furniture of the eighteenth century. This door-document was made by sticking three veneers some on the others, by meeting the threads of their wood. The leather of its slice is sandwiched between them.

The sea uses the veins of king wood. The sky is wild cherry. The sails are made of amaranth. Ebony earth. And walnut, box tree... 30 x 38cm.

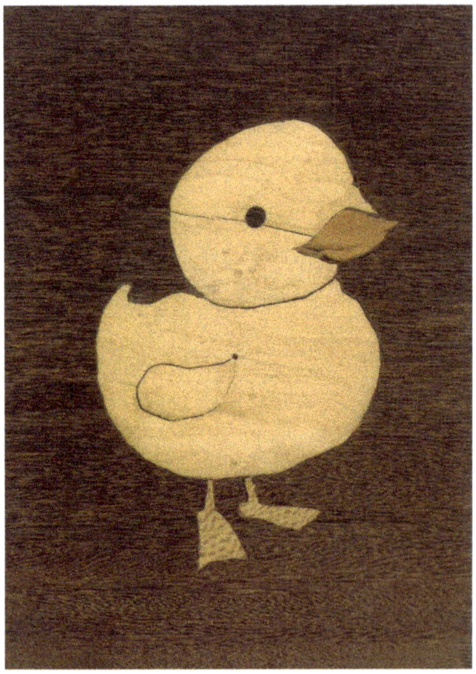
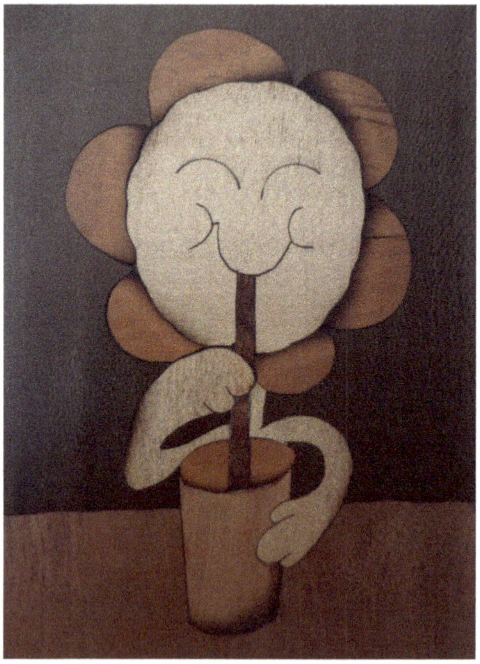
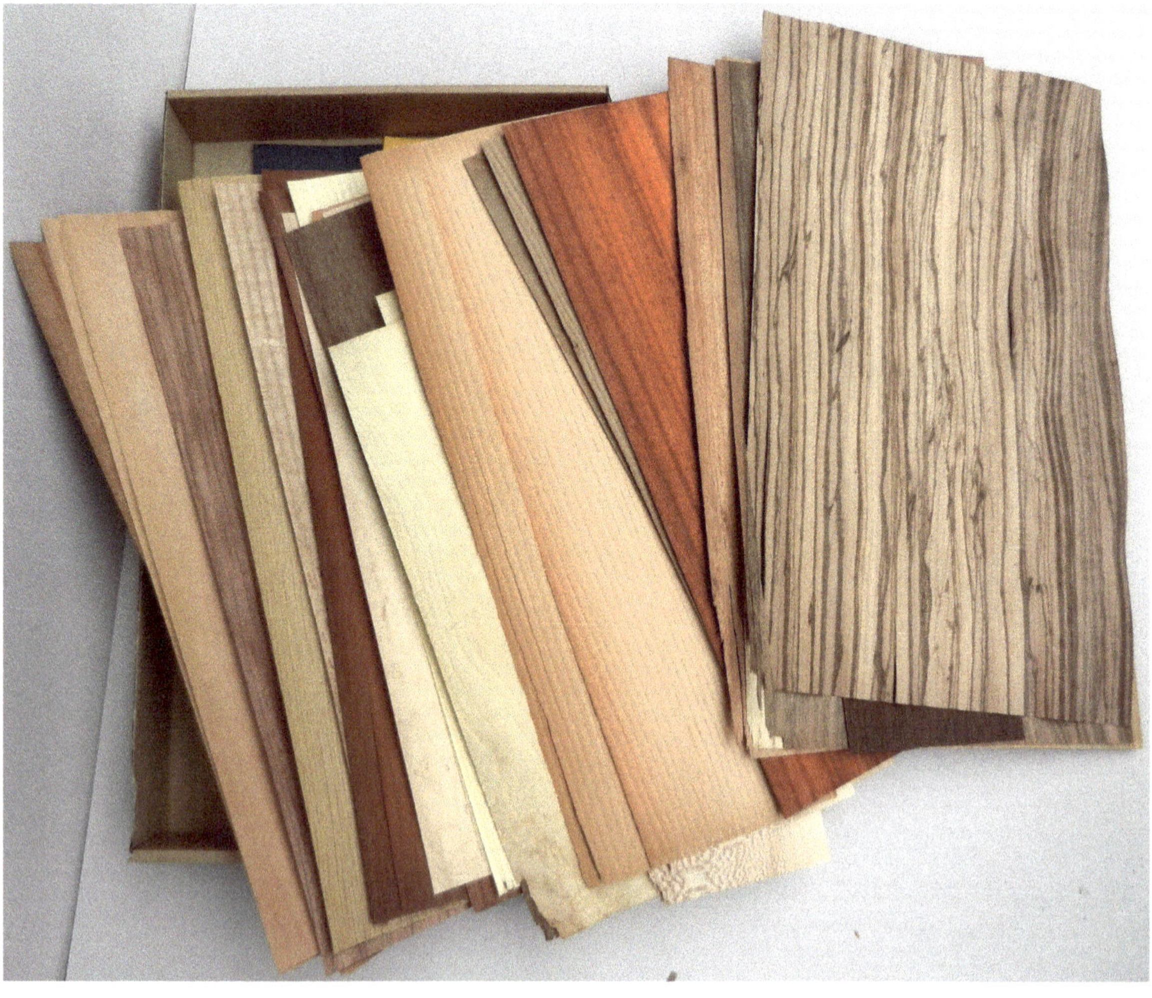

The easiest method

"by superposition"

For kids or leisure centers, it is advantageous because it is quick and asks fewer tools.

Example : a swordfish.

Yes kids can start young (my daughter Valerie cutting the duckling).

Material

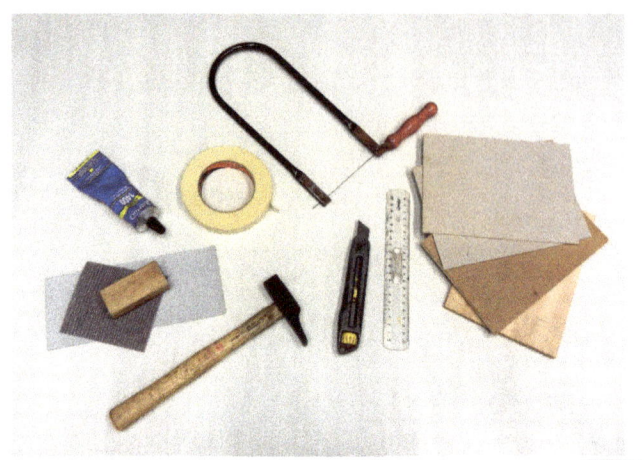

A fretsaw. On the left photo, you can see a hand saw which you can use to make small marquetry, but it is not easy to use. It is better to buy an oscillating arm power saw- the cheapest (102$) in a hardware store or a DIY store, completely equipped with its finest blade.

Work table : a table is enough. You can make marquetry in an apartment

Carton of 1,5mm of thickness, the frame stores sell some. Otherwise, calendars, covers of blocks… any flat cardboard will work.

Adhesive tape: it is a type of protection to paint its 2 cm large (of good quality).

A cutter, a rule and a hammer.

Laminate : you will obtain marquetry that you will stick on small panels of 21 x 15cm and of 8 to 10mm thickness. A hardware store with "wood in the cup" can prepare them for you.

Glue : neoprene glue in tube- liquid not gel.

Sandpaper.

Some **wax** or some **varnish).**

Wood veneers

These wood sheets cut in tree trunks have approximately one millimeter thickness. The simplest is to begin by buying a casket planned for marquetry such as the one who is in the picture, three pages higher. You will find on the internet traders who send it (by searching for veneer wood).

The caskets of veneers presented on page 10 has thirty different wooden essences : thirty papers 25 by 32 centimeters. They all have a number : a list that gives you names of thirty wooden sheets. The first sheet to the right is Zebrano. Like all the sheets in that picture, the color of the fourth sheet (red) is natural. It is of paddock, says "wood of coral". At the bottom of the casket, hidden under the others, there are 4 sheets of sycamore tinged in blue, red, yellow and green.

In principle these veneers are flat, but if one crinkles a little bit : flatten it by handing it to the iron, from both sides, without wetting it. If it is very deformed, see *complement on wood* page 57. If you want to buy veneers from the sheet to complete your casket, read the next chapter.

Choice for the swordfish

Ours is in wild cherry (orange-colored chestnut), rosewood (dark brown), sycamore (white) and amaranth (purpleheart).

Choose the sheets, but so that your marquetry is contrasted, in them four (or five) take a very dark and very clear.

A swordfish with different wood: bottom: sycamore tinged in blue, fins: pear tree and wild cherry, body: sycamore, backbone: rosewood.

Drawings. Photocopy in duplicate, that of the swordfish, by enlarging it to obtain a rectangle of 21 x 25cm (percentage to be indicated : dimension of the drawing that we want to obtain divided by that of the one that we photocopy, multiplied by 100).

Preparation of the veneers. Cut with the cutter, in each of your four sheets, a rectangle of 22 x 16cm (by putting the thread of wood lengthwise). To cut a veneer, it is enough to give two knocks of cutter along a ruler. Then press with one hand on the ruler and lift the other one: the wood breaks clear off.

Creation of the "package". Objective: stiffen the fragile veneers during the sawing of the swordfish, so that they don't burst under the teeth of the blade. Cut two cartons of 22 x 16cm. place the four veneers between these two cartons(they are "overlapped", where the name of this method). Close this package with adhesive tape on the two pieces of carton.

Split veneer. Recover the crack with adhesive tape. If all the rectangle of the veneer seems fragile, if it risks breaking during the cut of the swordfish, strengthen it by recovering it completely of adhesive tape. When forming the package, place the adhesive tape above, you will take it off when the marquetry will be glued on its support in plywood.

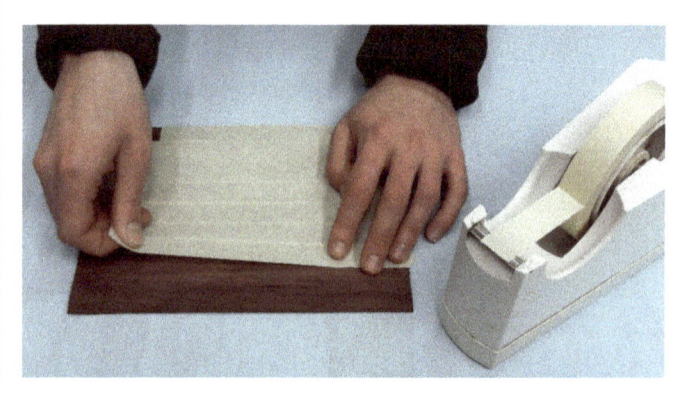

14

Stick the drawing of the swordfish on the top cardboard. Set the paper glue, neoprene or white with wood (put a little bit on that last one to not wet the paper too much, otherwise it would deform.)

Cutting. The swordfish drawing does not touch the edge of the package, thus it is necessary to reach it with the blade of the saw. Two solutions:
1. Enter the package where the drawing is the closest to the edge, the tail. It's what I did. We immediately maintain the crack with and edge of adhesive tape to stop the package from opening and from shaking during the cutting of the fish.
2. Drill a hole of 2mm on the drawing wherever you want, and commit the blade in the package.

A hand placed around the blade based on the packet to prevent it from vibrating. The other holds an edge and turns.

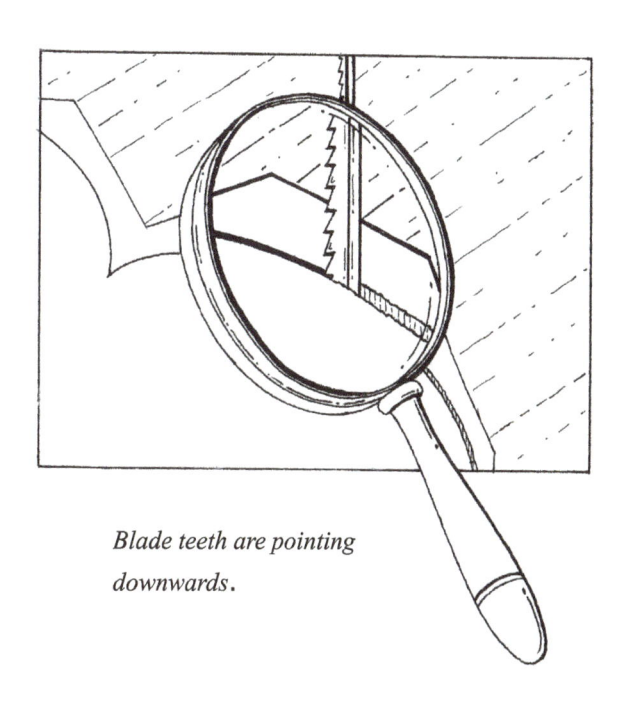

First hollow out the elements in the center of the package then saw the exterior of the swordfish.

In the angles, no operation of the blade is possible (it would damage swordfishes or their bottom). So to do the acute angles, quickly turn the package. It works: look at my marquetry, the rounding of the angles are barely visible.

If you go out of the lines of the drawing it is not a big problem, come back on it with a harmonious curb. The swordfish will be a little different…
Saw very slowly, it is the secret.

Blade teeth are pointing downwards.

Assembling

Open the package.
Assemble the marquetry by playing with the colors of the wood. There is always one we prefer.

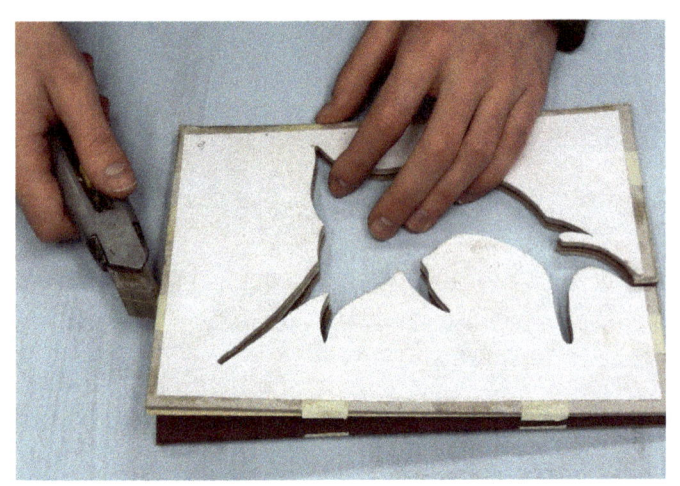

Maintain with adhesive tape the swordfish elements ; they adjust themselves perfectly because they were sawed at the same time.

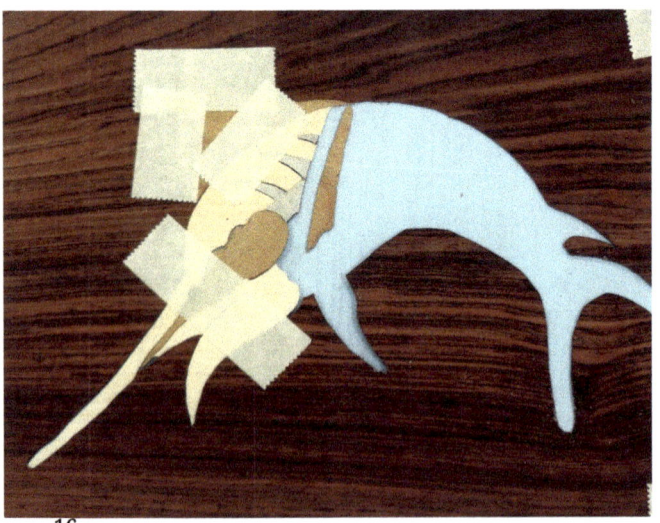

Collage

Stick "contact", the neoprene doesn't ask for tightening. It simplifies so much compared with the glue usually used. It (the neoprene) is great but demands the veneers to not be crinkled.

Turn marquetry upside down and put on that side, nets of glue.

With a piece of cardboard, immediately spread out the glue in a thin layer on the whole surface.

Also glue one of your small panels of plywood.

Wait ten minutes (the glue must not adhere when you touch it with a finger). Place the marquetry on the panel.

Wait half an hour so the glue has taken well, then remove the adhesive tape. Pull it slowly, as horizontally as possible.

Then turn the marquetry over and cut with the cutter the veneer which overtakes on the sides of the panel.

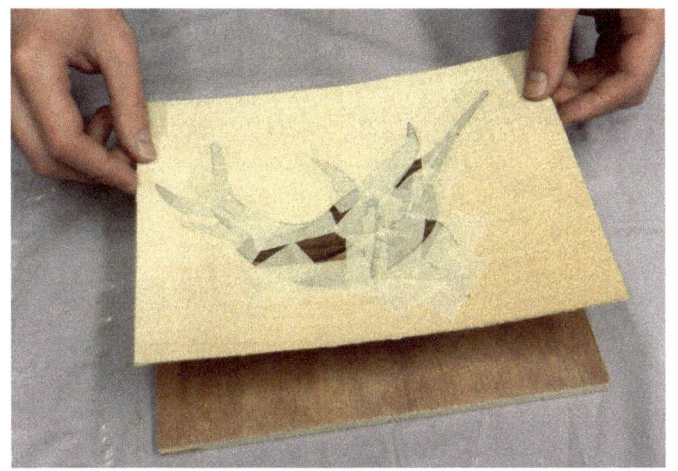

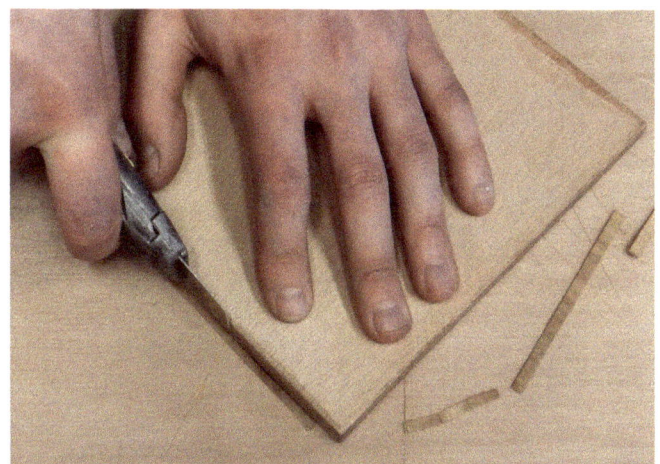

Press down hard with the heel of a hammer on the whole surface of the marquetry. Use the small side of the hammer to go in the hollows if a veneer is less thick than others.

There is no more that remains than to sand your works and to polish them r to varnish them.

For the finishing touches, go to page 42.

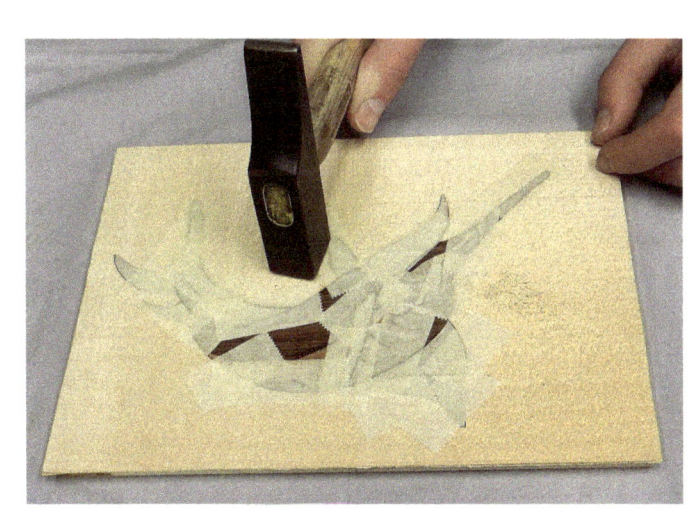

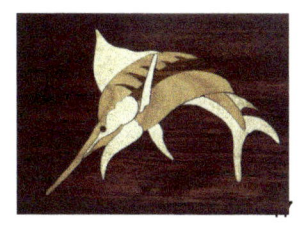

18

Use of this method for relatively complicated marquetry

It is enough to superpose more veneers in a package. So we limit ourselves to assemble one or two works if the colors of the others do not agree.

This picture contains seven different types of wood. It's the number close to a maximum, above that and a package becomes difficult to saw with a thin blade.
Bottom: Santos's rosewood. Feathers: pear tree and box tree are shadowed in the hot sand (see farther). The beak is in bone. And: sycamore, rosewood of India, elm burrs tinged in green. The pupil is an added nail after the collage. A bit unorthodox but effective… 22 x 30cm –drawing page 64.

A trick, to save some wood, consists to place in the package (which makes the size of marquetry) veneers just a bit bigger than the elements in which they will be cut.

To position veneers, we tape inside a photocopy of the drawing. I didn't put it here, to not hide the veneer at the bottom.

But these small pieces of superimposed veneers make the package not flat: it will be hard to hold it during the cut of the marquetry, it might vibrate.

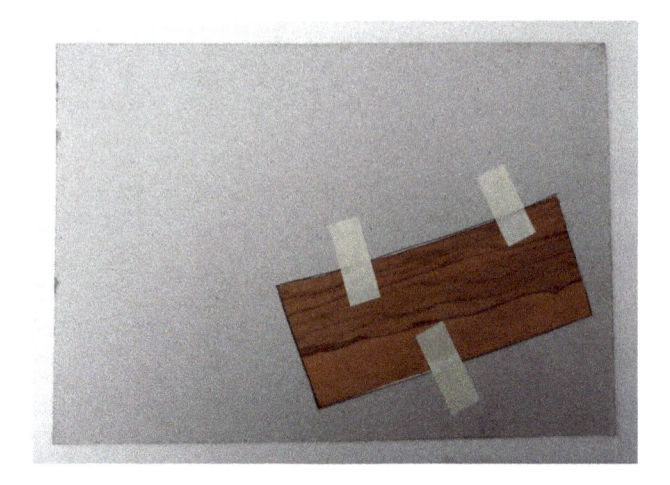

Rosewood, lime tree, plane tree, pear tree. The pupils are cut separately in a sheet of aluminum.
20 x 20cm.

A horse that runs fast. *It's one of the biggest marquetry jobs to make by overlapping (37 x 32cm), because during the cutting the package earths up in the fretsaw because of its limited arm size. Having said that, when we earth up, we unsettle the blade, we drill a hole somewhere else in the package (on the drawing); we engage the blade and continue to saw.*
Bottom: wood of violet and lemon tree. Horse: ebony. And: paddock, wild cherry, sycamore, and amaranth. The many internal cuts asked to drill small little holes on the plan and engage the blade.

The veneers were sawed by hand until the beginning of the nineteenth century.

Wood veneers

If you pursue the discovery of the marquetry –what I do not doubt –you will soon want to buy additional sheets.

No need to know much. You can find images of veneers on the internet. At a trader they are exposed on shelves. You can choose the one you find the prettiest on sight. Choose rather essences in the well-marked colors, among which the veins are very visible and which present drawings. Write their name on it with a chalk.

The sheets are sold in singles or by small piles of ten or twenty (less expensive in this case). The price is reckoned in square meter. Their dimensions can vary, from 30cm. if the sheets are too long (up until four French meters) ask the seller to cut them in half. At certain manufacturers, the veneer is proposed in two layers: 6 or 9 of millimeter. The thicker the better, but certain existing wood that in 6/10th, we do not go without it for so much. To straighten wrinkled veneers or strengthen those that is fragile, see the complementary chapter on wood, page 57.

Santos's rosewood and lemon tree of Ceylon.
The purchase of wood is for the marquetry artist is an exalting moment; he dreams of all the works he will create thanks to the beauties of new companions of workshop.

Fabrication of veneers

Its trees that create wood. Yes. But for us, transforming it into sheets is not an easy affair. Sawed manually, then with mechanical saws, sawed veneers are not used any more today, only except by restaurant owners of old furniture.

Clear-cut veneer: it's the one we buy for our works. This technique was invented in the middle of the nineteenth century. A ball (the trunk of the tree) is plunged into hot water to soften the wood. Then it is cut by a blade without teeth, in parallel sheets.

The sapelli mahogany dappled imitate the fur of the fox well of marquetry which we are going to make in some pages.

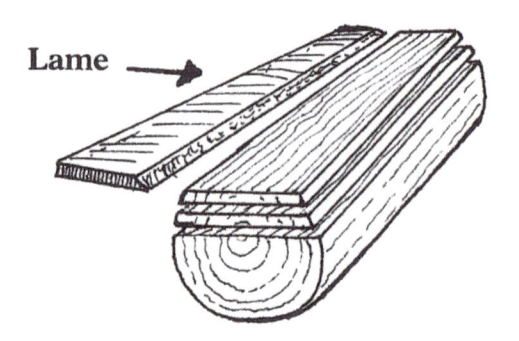

Unwound veneer: it's a different slicing. To make plywood, you need big sheets. The ball turns on itself and little like a pencil-sharpener it created an uninterrupted sheet. For us, it's interesting because it created original veining. The wood does not have regular seasonal veins, because the sheet "turns around". These effects are visible on the sapelli dappled mahogany, the speckled maple, certain works of Norway…

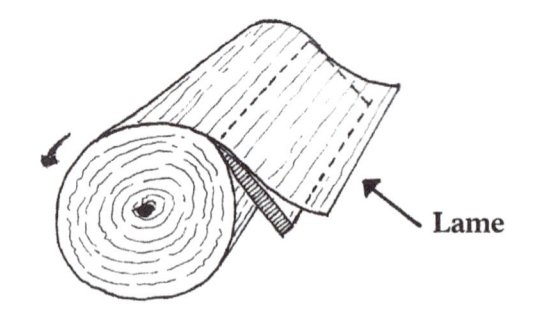

Different types of wood

Behind: tulip wood. Front: pear tree, ebony, apricot tree, ash tree, rosewood of India.

Local wood: (Europeans), elm, wild cherry, pear tree, yew, olive tree…

-**Imported wood**: nicknamed *wood of the islands* since the big conquests of the fifteenth century: ebony, mahogany, amaranth, rosewood, violet, lemon tree, sheen…

-**Colored wood**: the natural pallet is very varied but incomplete; we don't find wood really green, or blue. For the sixteenth century, to remedy it, marquetry artist color in their layers veneers by diving them in coloring agent. Often its sycamore, sometimes birch, the plane tree, the lime tree, of pear tree, charm, ash tree, speckled maple… on the other hand, light colored wood was discolored to make them very white.

Marquetry colors don not need to be completely makeshift; it is sometimes more fascinating to use more natural tones. Meanwhile, kids like bright colors… but what matters is that children like marquetry as they grow up, but they will stop asking for colored wood later on.

Interpretation of an English calendar. The bottom is made of sycamore, wood that's usually very light beige. This wide sheet, a rare one, is naturally pinkish and veined. The blue, green and orange are colored.   44 x 34cm

Particular effects

Burrs. Wood bumps engendered by sick trees or bothered by their growth (by a wire sometimes). The wood development is anarchy; there is a multitude of knots and very "messy" veining. Often beautiful.

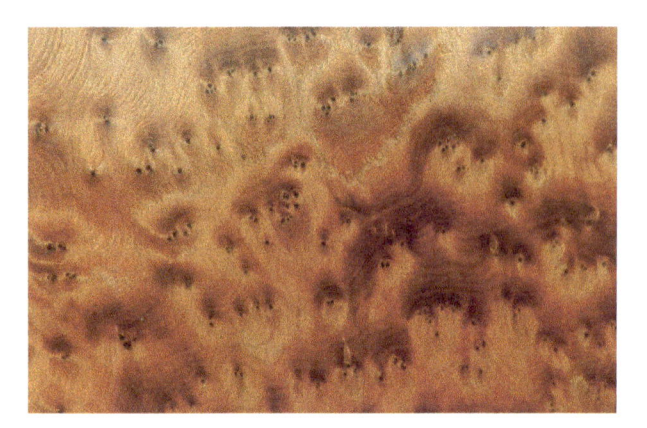

Tuya burrs

Brambles. From a branch or roots, the wood presents pretty rounded off, tortured veins. We can talk about "flame" mostly for the mahogany and the walnut. They resemble a rib cage or waves…

Flame of mahogany tree of Cuba

Meshed wood: the medullary beams in which the sap were cut by a blade during the veneer manufacturing. Each section forms a little circle in which the sap dried and formed a small mirror. These multiples mirrors that reflect the light and sparkle are called the stitch.

Meshed plane three, strangely interesting…the very thin stitch is hardly visible on the picture.

Watered wood: bright and dark reflections that are reversed when we move.

Watered satinwood

Peppered wood: This has strewed zones of black dots, like the sky in yew.

Speckled wood (on the left): the speckled mahogany of Cuba is magnificent. Here is a speckled maple, essence already used on the restoration (1815), then by cabinet makers Gallé and Majorelle around the middle of the twentieth century.

Banded wood: it presents the appearance of dark and light ribbons, without it being the veins of the seasons. In marquetry, it can represent a carpet, wallpaper, a lined fabric…

Waved wood: like its name indicates, it presents as bright waves in the surface, across the thread of wood.

Waved douka

Satined banded

You will see that you have, after two or three works, the technique to make marquetry like this one.
The girls and the unicorn. *Admire her dress of poplar burrs.   42 x 33 cm*

The comet, *contemporary marquetry. Burr elms, of vavona, thuya, Formosa... melted according to a method of sanding which we will see in volume 2. 40 x 30cm*

Very simple picture, the beauty resides in the choice of veining the three types of wood of the sky, the earth and of the tree. E. Kaplonski, Pologne.

Pen Duick, *from Eric Tabarly*

The sea is a great example of using flame of mahogany. The sky is made of rosewood from Madagascar melted with pink peroba.   80 x 54cm

Canaries' landscape. *21 x 15cm*

1. Wild cherry
2. Light blue birch from Norway
3. Avorio olivato
4. Tinged burr elm green (rocks) and tinged green sycamore(palm tree)
5. Light green colored sycamore
6. Tulip wood
7. Rosewood from Madagascar
8. Walnut
9. Louro-faia
10. Rosewood from India

30

Adam and Eve, *sky: plum tree. Body: white pear tree. Ground: yellow peroba and burr walnut. 33 x 27 cm*

Marquetry cutting "element by element"

You can start with this method without passing by "overlapping". To saw one by one every piece of veneer allows realizing grand marquetry, without limits of the number of wooden essences.

Birds: formosa burrs and meshed sycamore. Nest: meshed plane tree. Orangey flowers: pink peroba. Bottom: green ebony. Detail of marquetry, a drawing page 66.

The fox and the stork. The legend proposition :
1 wild cherry - 2 rosewood - 3 dappled mahogany - 4 flood - 5 avorio olivato
6 natural sycamore -7 louro-faia – 8 miss of Formosa - 9 box tree amarello
10 tulip wood - 11 amaranth -12 king wood -13 tulip tree -14 ebony green.

Material

Veneers. Every one of you will make a different marquetry than I did, and good, in dependence of the veneers that each own and their taste. For each wood, a number is attributed and noted on the drawing.

Eight **photocopies** of the drawing the fox and the stork enlarged to A4 format; 21 x 29,7cm.

Materials for swordfish: fretsaw, cutter, ruler, hammer, cardboard and adhesive tape.

Plus:
A small pointy pair of pliers to seize elements of the veneer. Most of the times we use a pair of tweezers but it can be a philatelist or medical.

A **drill** with a small wick of 2 or 3 millimeters.

Points with a flat head are better, around 10 x 0,7mm (if you find small nails a bit bigger it will do).

Optional: to shadow the elements, three centimeters of sand in a frying pan and one stove.

This material is used to compose marquetry. For the collage and its support and the finishing touch, go to page 42.

Training exercise

Before starting the fox and the stork, I recommend you to cut up this ace of spades to get comfortable with the method "element by element".

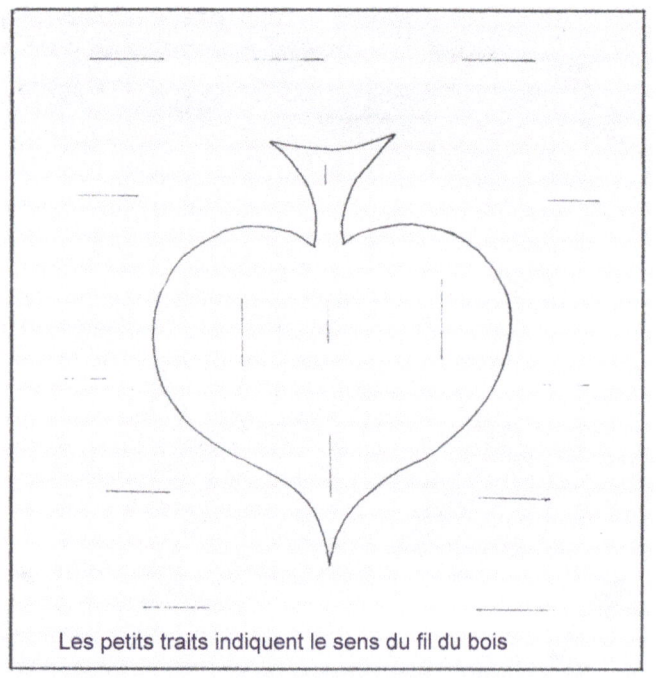

Les petits traits indiquent le sens du fil du bois

The little lines indicate the direction for the wood thread.

Photocopy the drawing in two examples, by enlarging it so the sides are 12cm. (percentage to indicate: the dimension of the drawing we want divided by the one we are photocopying times 100)

Veneers: this motive is composed of two elements: the bottom and the pike. Choose a light and dark wood. I took aniegre and mahogany from Africa (sapelli).

Forming two packages.

With a cutter cut two veneer squares: one for the bottom of 12 cm and for the pike 10cm. place each of them between two cardboard squares the same size. Close them with adhesive tape.

Cut with the cutter the paper pike at 2mm from the line.

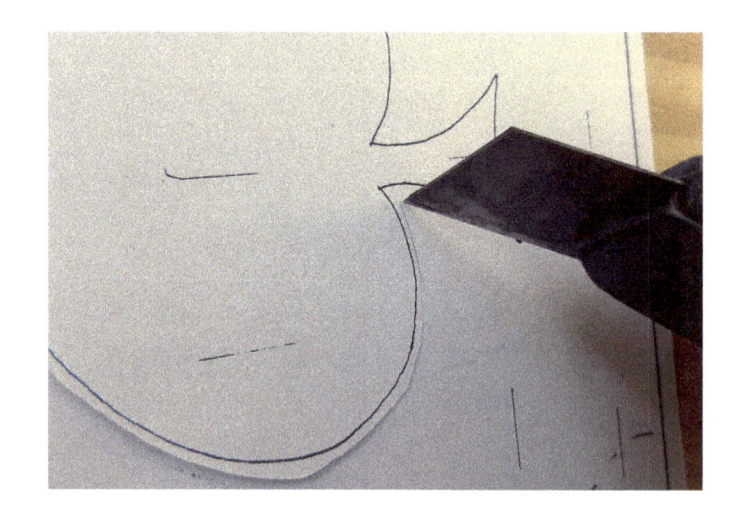

34

Glue the pike package with paper glue, or like here with white glue for wood that dries quickly: do not put too much to not wet the paper.

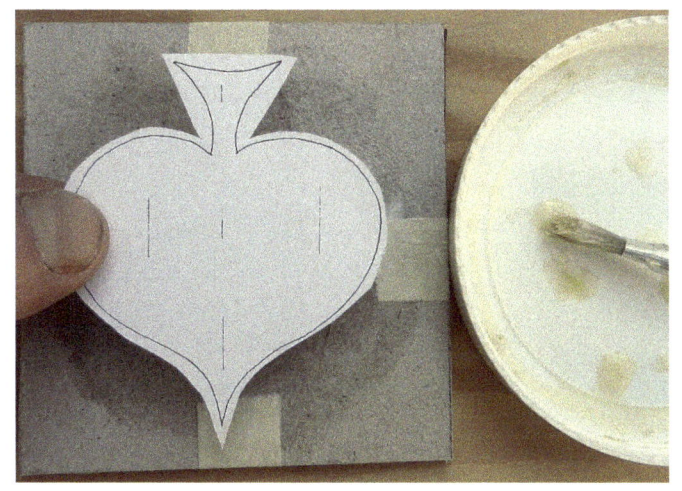

Do the same with the bottom. A little hole was made in this package to engage a blade, but you can't enter by cutting, it is only an exercise.

Cutting. Start with the pike. One hand near the blade, hold down the package so it won't vibrate. Use the other hand to turn it. Saw on the line, but very slowly so that nothing budges. In the beginning, the movement top to bottom of the blade gives us the impression to be "inhaled" forward: train yourself to master your progress by stopping and restarting slowly.

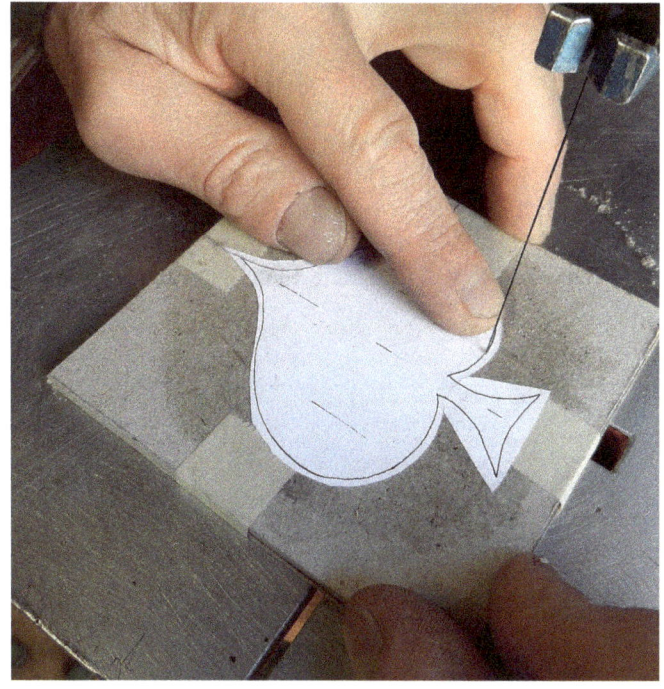

Contrary to the easiest "overlapping" method, to cut angles correctly you can maneuver the blade. I detail it next page, for a hollow it's the same as for a point.

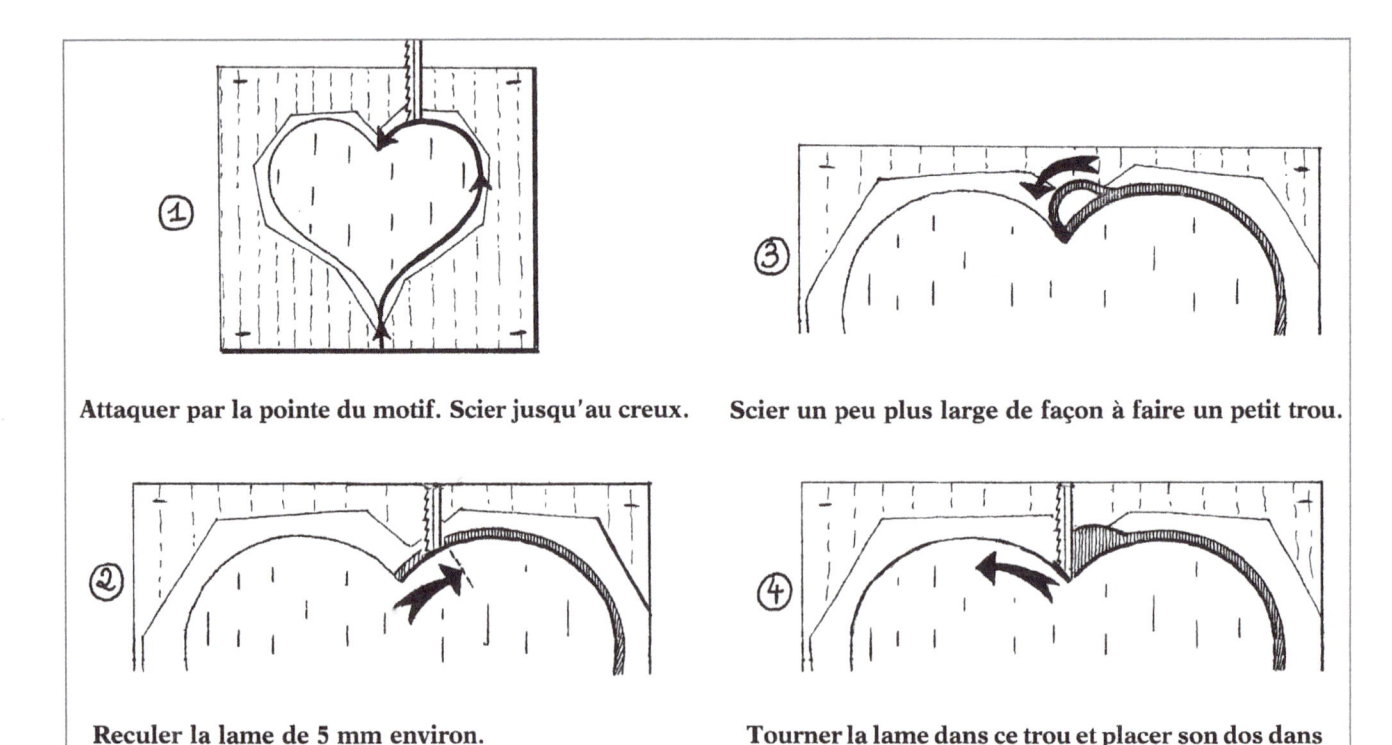

Attaquer par la pointe du motif. Scier jusqu'au creux.

Scier un peu plus large de façon à faire un petit trou.

Reculer la lame de 5 mm environ.

Tourner la lame dans ce trou et placer son dos dans l'angle. Repartir à angle aigu.

(1): start by the point of the motive. Saw until hollow. (2): push the blade back about 5 mm
(3): saw in a larger way to make a hole. (4): turn the saw in the hole and place the back in the angle.
Restart at the acute angle.

Beginners stop the saw in the middle of the maneuver and restarted; with practice it stays on. Careful, when you cut the bottom, do the correct maneuvers inside the pike (it will be emptied, so it can be damaged).

The first time will be difficult, but you will see that it will be easier with time, quicker than you think. We .aim for an "honorable" precision, by that I mean from a distance of one meter we do not see the joints, just its beauty.

This work by Hervé Foucat, since then excellent, this should remove inhibitions from you...

Le renard et la cigogne

Paper elements.

Cut with the cutter every piece of the drawing with a millimeter or two from the line. When we cut one drawing we might encroach on the others next to it, which explains why we need multiple copies of the drawing, we will add the eyes of the animals when marquetry will be glued on the plywood.

Regroup by wood essence your paper elements (those with the same number), by spacing them out with 2mm. the occupied surface, plus one centimeter around, will give you the size you need for the veneer.

To not forget any elements, we can gray out the elements we take one after another.

We call *martyred hold* the panel of plywood on which we cut the veneer and the paper, because it suffers instead of the table.

Packages formation

For each wood essence, make a package with two veneers, because you will cut matching marquetry a same time (one for you one for to offer). It's the biggest advantage of this method,, we can put maximum of six packages, until then it becomes hard to saw it. Make them around 20 x 15 cm, but just adapt them to the size of wood you have.

Fragile veneers: cover the cracks with adhesive tape. If the veneer is too fragile and risks breaking during the cutting, reinforce it by gluing adhesive tape all around (if it also crinkled, glue a paper on it as well, page 66). When making the marquetry, glue the adhesive tape on top, you can take it off when the marquetry is glued to the support.

Bottom: tulip tree, louro-faia. In the middle: gauged mahogany and violet wood. In front: amaranth.

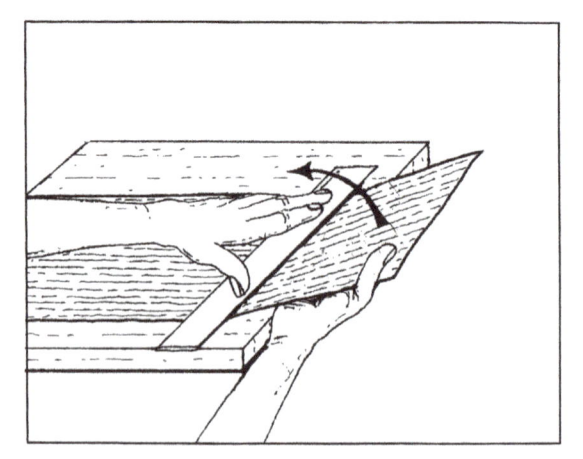

Glue the paper elements on packages :

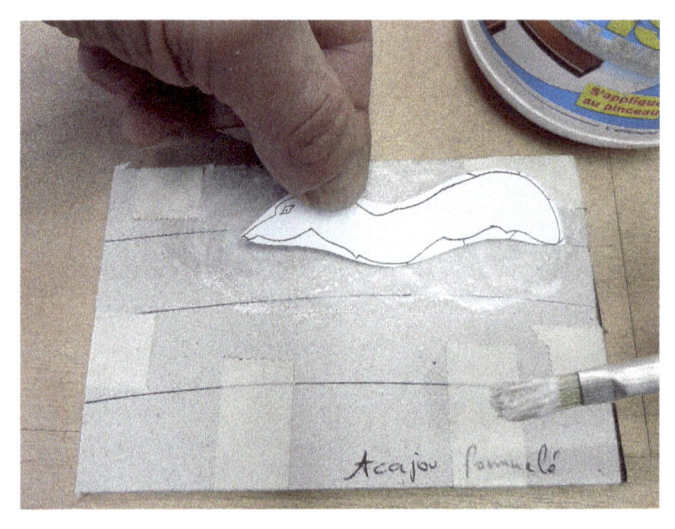

Cutting veneer: hit the ruler with the cutter and break it by lifting it.

Any glue will do. The white wood glue that dries quickly is best.

See on the picture above: -I noted the name of the wood on the top cardboard: dappled mahogany.

-I represented with lines of the wood thread. We principally put elements in their length.

Place the complicated element on the edge of the package, to cut it while the veneer is still united with the package. Put one or two veneer points around the elements to solidify the package.

"Seal" these points by pulling down with the hammer their extremities. Place the extremities on the top of the package so they won't attach the saw table (or cover them with an adhesive tape).

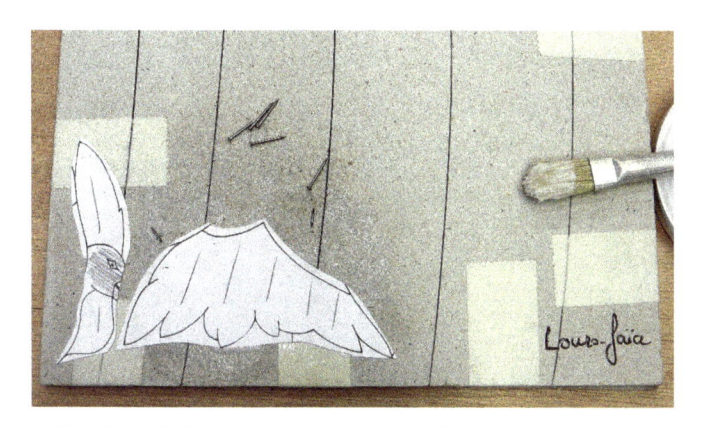

On this board, it's less shadowed, the vase is made of "wood of fault" to give the impression it was turned in the tour of pottery. The herbs are made of light and dark colored sycamore and not of tulip tree (slightly, naturally green). Violet wood, amaranth became chestnut-red with age.

I indicated the grain on the wings of the stork for not wrong by sticking them on the package. The large is placed across the wood for aesthetic reason.

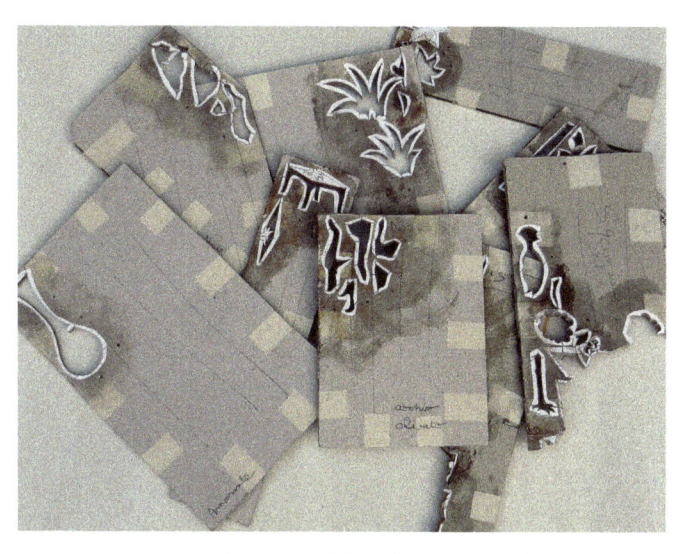

The packages used for other marquetries.

39

The bottom. The horizontal line being straight, assemble the sky and earth. Make both you're your bottoms a centimeter bigger than the drawing, which gives a 23 x 32 cm package.

To assemble well jointed two veneers, we stick pieces of adhesive tape across, then another on in length.

Solidify the bottom package with veneer points placed in the fox, the vase and the stork.

The point can then be folded again with the hammer afterwards. The extremity is then covered by a piece of adhesive tape so it won't stick to the saw table.

Cut

Elements: start with the side on the edge of the package. If you leave directly to the inside, the element will detach itself before you finished sawing.

"Engraving in the saw". The blade has to pass on all the lines of the drawing. It will therefore enter certain elements and this line will be visible. For example there are engravings in the tail and paws of the stork.

The bottom: drill two small holes: one in the fox and the stork. They will therefore engage the blade of the saw in the package.

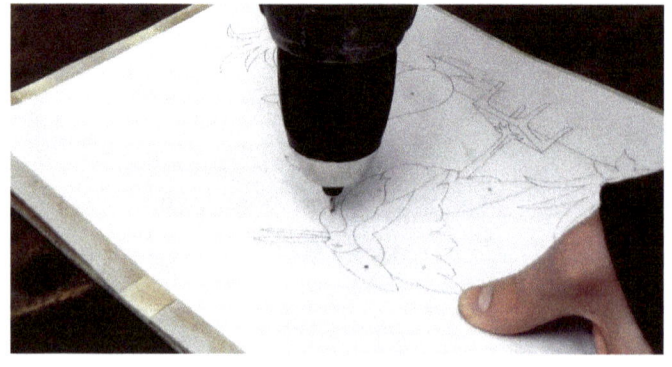

Careful, when cutting the bottom the blade maneuvers (for angles) are done in the inside of the elements. And do not recut the horizontal line! (You can erase it with a white-out on the drawing to avoid thoughtlessness.)

Stick an adhesive tape on and under the package as you cut. Sometimes it is best to remove and push away small pieces in the package that could move (although it is better to keep the big pieces to not weaken its rigidity).

Marquetry artist, assembling marquetry, drawn under Louis XVI's supervision by the cabinet maker Roubo in his book "art of the joiner" (1772).

Once the package opened, the bottom is ready to receive the elements.

Shadowing in hot sand

This stage is optional. Plunging a veneer element in very hot sand will lightly burn and tan it in gradation. It gives shadow and therefore a three dimensional impression.

You can tan it even more by leaving it in the sand longer or pushing it further down.

Place your veneers elements by reproducing the exploded drawing, to locate them and seize them easily.

You can use any type of sand, the thinnest being better (it'll suffice to sieve it with a sieve).

Three centimeters thickness in a pan.

Heat it with a regulated stove set to maximum. Try by plunging a fall of veneer held at the end of a thin metallic pair of pliers.

When the right temperature is achieved, lower the stove: thermostat 4 or 5 on 6. A gas stove also works.

Shape the sand in a hole or bump to form the same shape as the element.

Wood shadows more or less quick depending of the essences, thus the surprise we could have of burning one of them.

The more the elements are horizontally plunged in the sand, the more the shadow will be laid out. Move it often so that the limit will be degradable.

The shadowed and assembled marquetry (adhesive tape is behind.)
A wooden picture of less than one millimeter of thickness.

The heat deforms wood but it will flatten during the collage of marquetry. However if the veneer sticks out too much from the sand, place a heavy object on it so it will even out as it cools down.

During the sanding of the marquetry, the superficial part of the shadow will disappear (especially for hard wood that can't shadow easily). Don't hesitate to frankly shadow.

Don't forget if the color of the wood fade over time, the shadowing won't budge: it's a good reason to fix this hard step but essential, which gives it a three dimensional, contrast and life to the work.

The shadowing gives the three dimensional to the flowers.

Assembling the marquetry

Under the heat of the sand the wood shrunk. Wait a few hours after having shadowed so that they regain their size by absorbing the humidity (wet wood inflates). If an element shrinks too much, barely moisten the hollow side. If it extends too much, heat the convex face with a hair-fryer or thermal cleaner.

Maybe you will tell yourself : shoot, nothing fits. But really, by looking closely you will see that only some harshness prevent the elements from coinciding. Take them back slightly with the cutter or sand their edges with sandpaper or nail file: suddenly everything fits. If the veneers move away (the wood deforms a little bit) play with the elasticity of adhesive tape to move them closer together.

All the marquetry artists rectify some elements while assembling their marquetry.
I stuck sandpaper on a small board; it's practical and allows to "raising" the edge of a straight veneer.

Board veneer

Support: two plywood panels of A4 12mm in thickness.

Neoprene glue: its immediate grip has the advantage of not needing to be tightened, which simplifies it. It's very good glue, you can trust it. But the veneers have to be flat, or almost. For this size marquetry, very small, you can use a tube (liquid, not gel, see first chapter). Glue in a jar: spread with a paint brush, or a piece of cardboard made into a spatula, a thin layer of glue, regularly on the surface of the marquetry. Do the same on the plywood. Wait ten minutes. Apply them. Press on the veneers with a hammer.

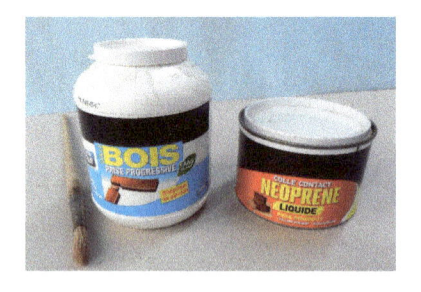

White glue- material: prepare it in advance because you need to tighten the marquetry the second it touches the glue. Otherwise the veneer stretches out while humidifying and overlap each other.

-holds of tightening: many plywood a little bit bigger than the marquetry, being around 23 x 32cm and 15mm of minimum thickness.

- A 23 x 32mm cardboard
- A plastic paper. The one you use to recover your books will be perfect.
- Six good clamps
- White glue with normal or rapid grip, no matter.

Here the plywood support is bigger than the marquetry; you'll need to cut it afterwards.

Collage

Coat the panel with a layer of glue (don't put any on the marquetry or the veneer will crinkle). Place the marquetry on top. Cover it with the plastic paper and the cardboard that will be used to level the veneers. Place a tightening hold on and under. Squeeze 12 hours for normal glue, 2 hours for quick glue.

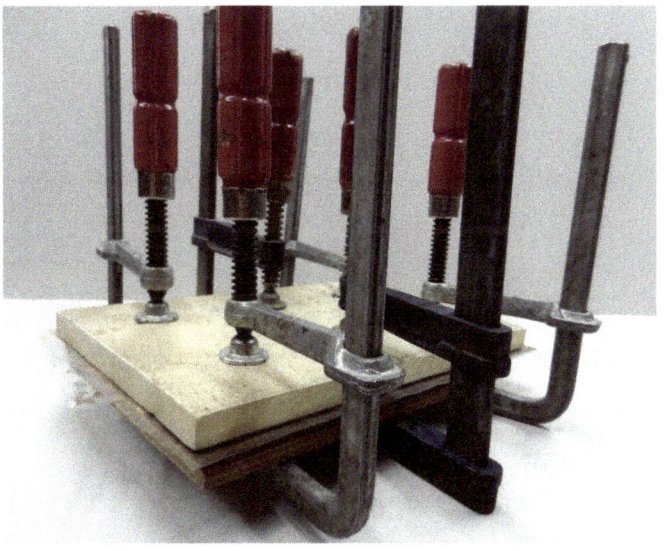

Advise: before gluing your marquetry, cover the edge of the panels with adhesive tape to protect it from the glue. (It'll help you avoid that you have to scratch it with a rapper or a cutter.)

Remove the adhesive tape

Loosen the plastic and let it dry for half a day with normal glue and half an hour for the quick glue.

Raise the tape as horizontally as possible. Wood scissors are useful to seize it, or just the point of a cutter. We can also use a thermal cleaner or a hair-dryer because adhesive tape removes itself better if it is slightly heated (a very little bit).

If the fibers of the wood tear away, grab the adhesive tape on the other side.

Inlay of the eyes

Over laying a small element when the marquetry is stuck allows us to adjust it precisely. Cut a diamond shaped eye out of rosewood for the stork or sycamore for the fox (but beforehand, so that it won't burst cover the veneer with adhesive tape).

Place the eye on the animal. Keep it in place with, for example the point of a pencil. Mark the outline with four strokes of the cutter. Here's a trick so the eye won't slip: stick it with double-sided transparent tape on the animal's head (it can be found in stationaries). Remove the eye and finish the notch with a cutter.

Put a drop of glue in the accommodation; sink the eye by pressing down on it with the heel of your hammer.
Drill the pupil with a millimeter drill. Fill the small hole by planting a piece of veneer cut with a cutter.

Veneer songs of the board

Cut with the cutter pieces of veneer that overtakes on the edge of the corners, the "songs, of the panel. Level them with sand paper on a wooden hold.

To finish we can simply darken them with a walnut stain tan or paint it chestnut. But perfectionists will take time to glue wild cherry strips which will give the illusion that the support is made of massive wood.

Cutting the strips. On the right the clamp hold the ruler (whichever bracket or falling wood serves as a ruler).

Prepare four strips of veneer with a width of two millimeters more than the thickness of the panel (14mm).

Place a layer of neoprene glue on the song. Spread it with a piece of cardboard. Same thing on a strip.

Wait ten minute. Apply the strip on an already glued side. Squeeze it tight with a wooden hold.

Cut what overtakes on the side in width. Finish leveling the sandpaper strip. Stick the second side, etc.

Cut each extremity of the strip: begin the break of a sudden blow from the cutter then a clean blow with a sanding hold (a piece of wood of 45 x 90 mm).

Veneer saw, or cutter works too.

Finishing

Sanding. Use sand paper (or like on the photo of the abrasive cloth). Of rather big grains: around 120: then medium: 180; then thin or very thin: 240 to 320. Every sanding erases the lines of the previous sandpaper.

Start with a sanded hold (a simple piece of wood). When the veneers are leveled, finish with sand paper, without hold, with fingertips. Change the direction of the sanding multiple times to not dig at one point in the veneer.

To hold the marquetry together, two less thick laminated r \that are fixed with clamps.

Polish. The marquetry suddenly gains color! They may be very bright on the moment but they will fade out when the polish dries. Pass with the brush of the furniture polish (mixture of beeswax and turpentine essence) for furniture. Wipe the surplus on a rag. Make it shine with a wool rag that does not go fluffy. Re-polish a week later.

Varnishing accentuates more the colors and differences of the vein in the wood than polishing does. Buy a cabinet-making varnish colorless sheen. Place two spaced out layers of six hours. Slightly sand with thin sand paper and apply a third layer.

Tricks: if your saw is not deep enough to cut the grand package at the bottom:

-when you get stuck on its arm, unmount the blade and engage it farther on the drawing of the marquetry (by drilling a small new hole): you can keep cutting.

-nice drawing in the bottom in multiple parts to not have a big element to saw, like the one of Dr Duck, made of ash tree, speckled maple and rosewood:

There is more than just wood in the materials: bone tin and mother-of-pearl, materials about which I speak about in the second volume.   60 x 54 cm

For the three A, B, C veneers on the bottom fit nicely: make one of them, C, bigger than centimeter. Assemble A and B. slide C under them; trace their edges by guiding yourselves on theirs. Cut them with the cutter, the game is played.

Advice and ideas

Before sawing a complicated a bottom, to not get it wrong : color the small parts of the bottom that will remove itself and that has to be preciously guarded.

In blue: the pieces of the bottom that you have to put aside (navigational instruments).

Plywood holds with adhesive tape.

Fretsaws with an oscillating arm **use only a few teeth from a blade**. Cutting 5mm when it's worn out, with pincers, move the teeth that saw, that'll delay the moment you have to replace it.

Another idea to move the teeth: put on the table of your saw plywood, split in front by a saw, to slide the blade. This plywood is also advantageous to reduce the light (the hole) of the table of the saw, to cut the small elements.

These **magnifying-glasses** of a jeweler magnify by four, which helps to be precise to cut and assemble elements. They are optional !

Rub the table of the saw with a piece of paraffin wax or of soap that allows the packages to revolve simpler.

Shadowing "with a shovel" (in abundance). To shadow the middle of an element, place hot sand with a spoon.

A foot switch inserted between the saw and the power socket allows stopping the blade easily to make maneuvers in angles.

The space between the elements.

Sticks of colored wax sold under the name of "polish in recork" in hardware shops.

Tablets to place your elements: a plywood rectangle and four baguettes stuck or nailed.

A few hollow joints are visible ?
-<u>Polished marquetry</u>: wait for the polish to dry (or accelerate the drying with a hair-dryer). Fill joints by rubbing above with a stick of wax beforehand warmed in your hands. Remove the surplus by rubbing with a rag. Polish the marquetry.
-<u>Varnished marquetry</u>: fill joints after the first layer of varnish. Rub multiple times with a clean rag to degrease the wood before passing a second layer of varnish.

Engravings made with a cutter. After gluing the marquetry on its support, sand a little bit to clean the veneer. Draw with a pencil the engraving you will do. Pass two times with the cutter, in V shape, on line made by the pencil. Finish sanding. Recork the furrow with a wax stick to be recorked: the engraving appears.

The petals and leaves are lightly engraved, and like often in the eighteenth century, there's ink in the engravings to mark them. It's difficult to restore marquetry without erasing them, we can't sand it, or barely. ("Happiness of the day" on page 6.)

To not mistaken the small elements that look alike, give them a letter on the drawing.

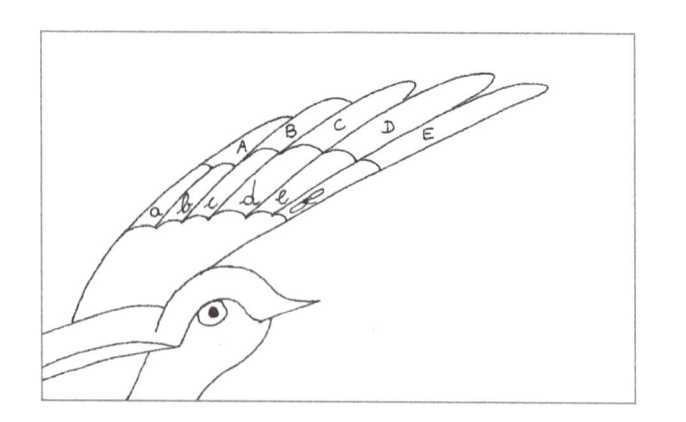

Raise the precision of the marquetry. Assemble al the elements by pressing them together as much as you can, without using the space that remains for the last one. The trick is not to use the last element but to recut exactly using the space that is left. This is how:

Place a piece of paper under the marquetry. Trace the location of the element that has to be cut again. This drawing is used as a paper element: stick it to the package of wood that is concerned. Saw the new element. Do not forget to shadow it is necessary.

Statement of the new, well-adjusted element. In dotted lines: the whit piece of paper that was slid under the marquetry.

A bridge hold will allow tightening the middle of the marquetry when we don't have a rather deep clamp.

52

A vibrating sander will help gain time, by using it lightly to not refine the veneer (120 bead pretty quickly, then 180). Since it heats the wood, let it cool down time to time so the wood won't unstick itself.

Keep it flat, train yourself before with plywood if you are not used to the machine.

Element made "by superposition" used in the marquetry "element by element".

To make the lined fabric from the vest of the carpenter, I made the packet with purple wood veneer and rosewood. I cut within them curve strips, that I then assembled by alternating one light, one dark… then I made another package with a new veneer: "lined fabric" in which I cut the vest.

This method allows making it much easier complicated boards.

Marquetry page 7. The optimist carpenter.   *60 x 83 cm*

Framing marquetry

Here is a method that gives perfect cuts to angles :
Cut four veneer strips. Fix a strip on the side of the marquetry. Cut the angles of 45 degrees by placing your ruler on the diagonal of a square whose side is the small side of the marquetry. Do the same with the strip on the opposite side.

Place a third and fourth strip under the first ones. Tape them.
Cut the angle by sliding the cutter along the first cuts.
Maintain the angles with adhesive tape so it won't open during collage of the marquetry.

This thin frame is called "composed net".

Nets sold by the meter by veneer sellers.

Another idea: change shape.

55

Medaillon

Make up the marquetry on a regular ebony bottom (drawing page 67).

Make a package composed of rosewood paper and the marquetry. But before closing the package, trace a horizontal line and a vertical line on the marquetry as well as on the photocopy of the drawing: lines that pass on the exact same place for both.

Put these lines on the cardboard above the package. Close the package and stick on the top of the drawing by overlapping the lines.

Drill a small hole in the oval drawing.

Engage the saw blade and cut the oval ("by superposing").

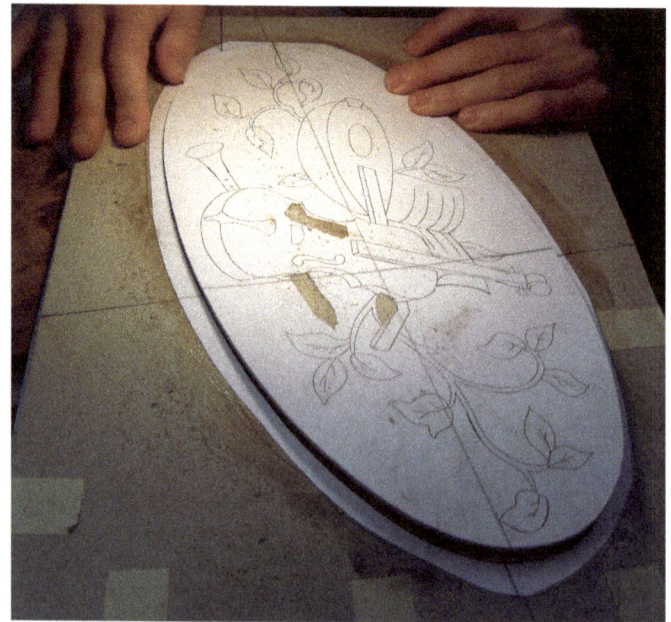

56

Net (optional).
To have the necessary space to put the net, open the sides of the bottom made of rosewood in the direction wood thread.

Input the net by maintaining it with adhesive tape.

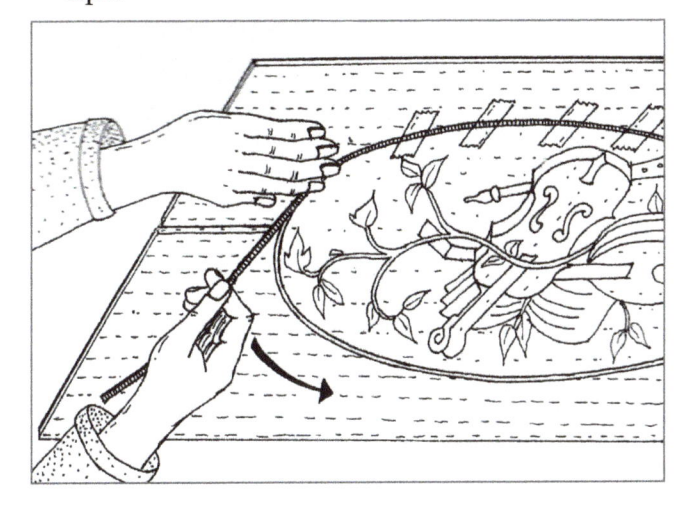

Now you just need to fabricate small rosewood strips to "restore" the cracks on the sides. For the drawing, it's easy: place a rosewood veneer under a crack and trace with a pencil the strip that's missing. Cut it with a cutter.

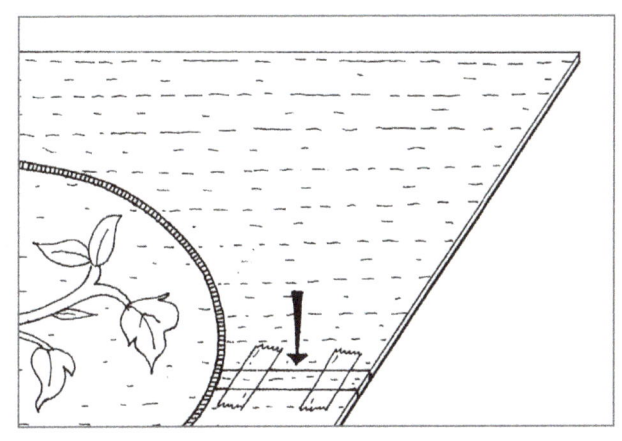

Trace an ellipse.
The oval in the medallion is generally an ellipse. Plant two nails, attach a thread. Trace while pulling on the pencil with the thread :

The drawing

To obtain an ornament that he'll paint with brief blows of a paintbrush made by the nature, the creator won't need to know how to paint. He's around a lot of graph ideas that he can interpret: rug ornaments, comic books, sketches, pictures, publicities… he just needs to retrace it by simplifying, and by dividing the elements.

Thanks to a photocopier, the trick to gain a precise drawing is to enlarge the original a lot before retracing, then reducing your drawing. It also refines the lines. Try the cat page 20, for example.

If the drawing is big enough, it will be enough to link several photocopies with tape.

Reducing difficulties.

- Sharp angles need saw blade maneuvers. B will be easier to cut than A:

- Drawing engravings with the saw on an element can help avoid slitting it in many pieces.

- Avoid drawing numerous internal cuts because it is bothersome to unsettle the saw blade often to engage it in packages. It is enough to link the elements together. If we add a puddle in the board the fox and the stork, there is only one hole to drill in the bottom not two.

Drawing from a chocolate cereal box.

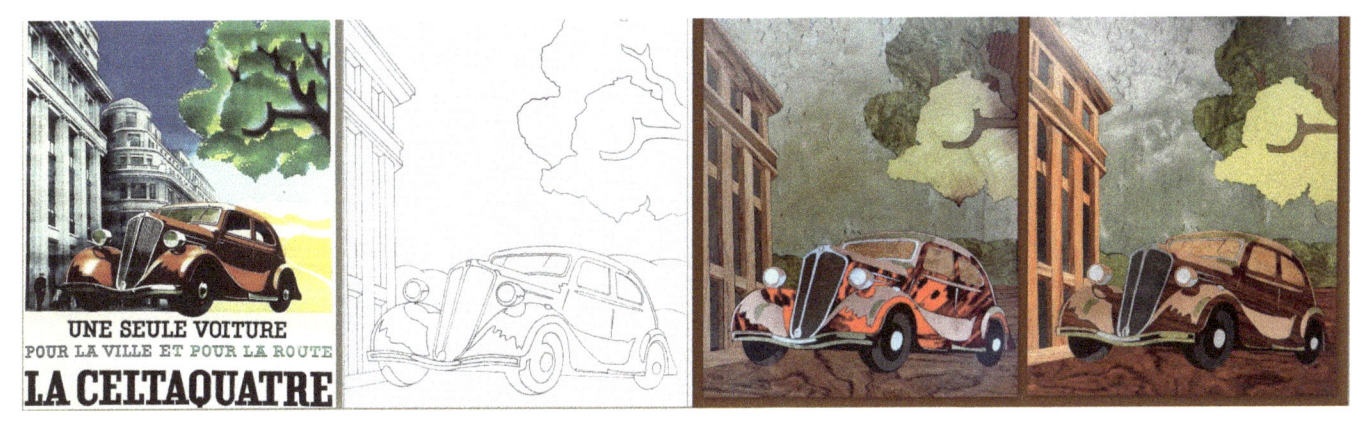

The drawing is retraced from an ancient publicity. The two versions of a work are cut at the same time by putting two different veneers in the package of the body of the car: rosewood and tortoise colored in red (method "element by element").   40 x 28cm

Ornament in amaranth cut by overlapping on this attractive worker stuck in magnifying glass of ash tree (restoration time, feet in lyre.)

**Anita Jany
Battaszek.
Germany**

60

Barry Freestone marquetry. England

Work exposed at International Meetings of the Marquetry (RIM) at Versailles.

Wood complement

Color classing

This list will help you know what color veneer to buy. You will have without doubt the occasion to complete it :

White (or almost): sycamore. Holly. Charm. Lime tree. Poplar. Birch. Chestnut tree. Ash tree. Beech. Plane tree, fir tree.

Yellow (light yellow): French box tree. Amarello box tree (bright yellow). Yellow peroba. Samba. Olive tree. Lemon tree. Zapatero. Sheen. Hawthorn.

Greenish: ebony green. Tulip tree. Guaiac. Warmed wood like poplar having rotted on the wet ground.

Red. Mahogany. Doka. Padouk (drink coral). Courbaril. Larch. False mahoganies of Africa (sipo, sapelli). Red martinmas. Sequoia (that gives magnifying glass of vavona).

Pink: tulip wood (pink rosewood). Aniegre. Coubaril. Serviceberry tree. Cedar of the Lebanon. Sob. Apple tree. Sheen. Pink ivory (very lively, almost red). Red cedar (huge thuya).

Orange color: wild cherry. Sheen. Mahogany from Cuba. Yew. Pink pine peroba. Pitchpin. Heather, red pear tree. Alder.

Purple: king wood. Amaranth (purpleheart). Rosewood. Sheen.

Chestnut: the list is long: walnut, oak, rosewood. Teak. Louro-faia. Chestnut. Zebrano. Plum tree. Elm. Bilinga. Larch. Affair.

Black. Ebony. Green ebony. Wenge wood. Wood of guaiac heart (iron wood). Lakeside oak, darkened by a long soak in water.

The "island wood"

Imported from Latin America since the sixteenth century, then later also Indonesia and Africa, the balls went up the Seine by boat until Paris to feed those whom we called "joiners in ebony", of which inlaid furniture make the admiration of the entire world.

The "lemon tree" (citronnier) witch gives **satinwood,** is not our fruit tree (of which beige wood loos like that box tree), it's from America and is named this way for its color lemon yellow. We called it "lemon wood" (bois de citronnier).

The **rosewood** from Brazil is beautiful and hot chestnut red streaked with black thread, and yet Roubo find it sad we wonder why.

The rosewood from India and Asia are darker and more united.

Tulip wood and **king wood** are of course not wood of our flowers (rose et violette) but varieties of rosewood from America, of pink (rose) and purple (violette) colors.

Amaranth (purpleheart) is very current as a frame of pink wood, on which it cuts a bit too much, which Roubo estimates difficult. His purple turns into chestnut when it ages.

Mahogany: this tree is a sort of walnut. This time our cabinet maker is right, it is sometimes not easy to differentiate a mahogany bleached by the time by time of a beautiful walnut. Some furniture Louis XVI are in walnut tinged in red to imitate the mahogany.

Before we said: wood "in cashew", sap of a shrub which we soaked the extremity balls during the transport by boat. There are two families in America: the Cuba and the Honduras. The "chestnuts" of Africa: big Bassam, sipo, sapelli… are not from the chestnut family, but their wood pulls towards the red.

Sheens are a magnificent wooden family of America the fine stitch of which sparkles. They can vary from yellow bright gold with brown made purple via the red; we can mistake them sometimes, even experts, with a lemon tree, pink wood or amaranth. This wood always seem transparent which is actually the principal beauty, written by Roubo, conquered can be by the variant called affair, of one beautiful meshed brown speckled with black..

Chest of drawers Louise XVI in sheen.

The ebony, feminine name. Its black sometimes reflects red and green. Those from Madagascar have white veins. The sapwood is white (wood near the bark of the tree), the black and white contrast is used to decorate plated furniture. Green ebony (Guyana and Brazil), in reality the ipe has a very dark unrefined, brown bead pulling toward green. We sometimes call it false ebony.

The paddock, called coral wood, is red but much like amaranth turns towards chestnut in the light. In Africa, in rich and saturated with water soil, it grows quickly and is therefore tender and its bead is not very thin.

Let's not denigrate the African essences in general. The **pink ivory** was called royal "wood" by the Zulus. Only the chief and his sons could own any. Anybody contradicting this law was sentenced to death, which I understand because of the heart of the wood of the tree, magnificently thin, it shines without even waxing it, just by polishing it! Its red won't fade with time.

We wet the wood to show what it will look like after being varnished.

The original wood, like **palm trees** interest us very much. It looks like a snake's skin:

This veneer shows the thin lines of the saw since it is sawed veneer. The ball is too small to be cut. To mix sawed and clear-cut in marquetry is no problem at all.

Hawthorn sawed in wood: "in sausage form". This bright yellow wood that comes from a bush makes pretty petals of flowers. You need to glue it on a paper before cutting it.

The more a tree has a hard time growing, in poor soil, with a little water, the more the wood will be hard, thin and prettily tortured.

Instead of cardboard, traditional makers use tender wood with 2 or 3mm thickness, to make their veneer packages. Often Samba :

The packages are closed with small points instead of adhesive tape.

Fruit basket and flowers on the bottom, in a rosewood frigate. Chest drawers in transition Louise XV - Louis XVI.

Tanned wood: sky in speckled blue maple, hair in discolored aniegre, blue and green sycamore sea, black pear tree. Natural wood: arm and face of pear tree, yellow docker in box tree amarello, white sycamore for marine animals.

Fragile or crinkled veneers

Most often we use veneers like this. Sometimes to level the sheet that would be slightly crinkled we iron it on both sides, without wetting it.

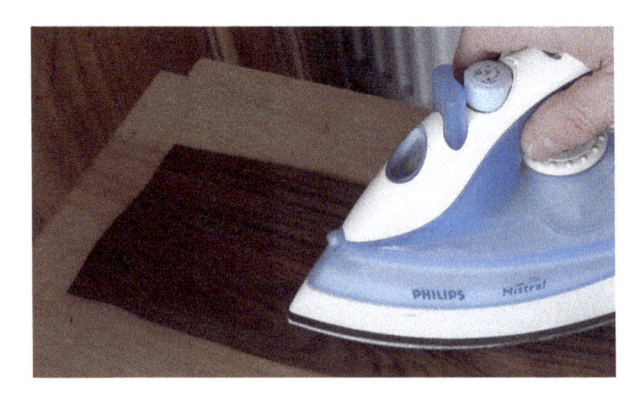

But if the wood is too deformed, you need to squeeze it between two hot metallic plates (or glue paper on it, see next page). Plates of whatever metal, or zinc or aluminum of 8 to 10 millimeters thickness, sold by cut at metal traders. Heat both plates on the stove. The best temperature 100 degrees, is obtained when drops of water we throw on them start crackle. Hotter, and they would blacken the wood when burning it.

Don't put any adhesive tape on the veneer, it would melt. You'll maintain the cracks later.

Progressively tighten to leave the wood time to become supple without splitting. If the veneer is breakable, moisten it with prerequisite, a little, with a sponge. Leave under a press a day.

We can reposition two or three sheets at the same time.

Un-tighten. If the veneer is still humid, tighten it again, between even more journal papers, let it dry for half a day then change the paper and tighten once again.

Place the veneer under a big dictionary so it won't deform again.

Reinforce the veneer. We know that adhesive tape can be used to reinforce small surfaces, or simply not split or fragile veneer. In the case of fragile or easily broken wood, magnifying glass for example, we stick a paper on it. This paper will be removed during the finishing step by wetting it or scraping it. Coat the veneer with wood glue and rest the paper on top.

Sticking paper on deformed veneers redresses it in general. Useful if you do not have metal plates.

Place it between two plastic sheets and squeeze between two plywood holds, if the wood is not too breakable. If it's stiff, deformed and breakable, which is rare, it needs to be squeezed with two warm metal holds. That forces us to replace the plastic (that could melt) with journal paper. These holds can't be too hot, to distort the glue: we just need to be able to hold them with our hands.

The dictionary technique.

Marquetry drawings

Enlarge the ornaments to the dimension you wish (and in dependence of the veneers you have, especially for the bottom).

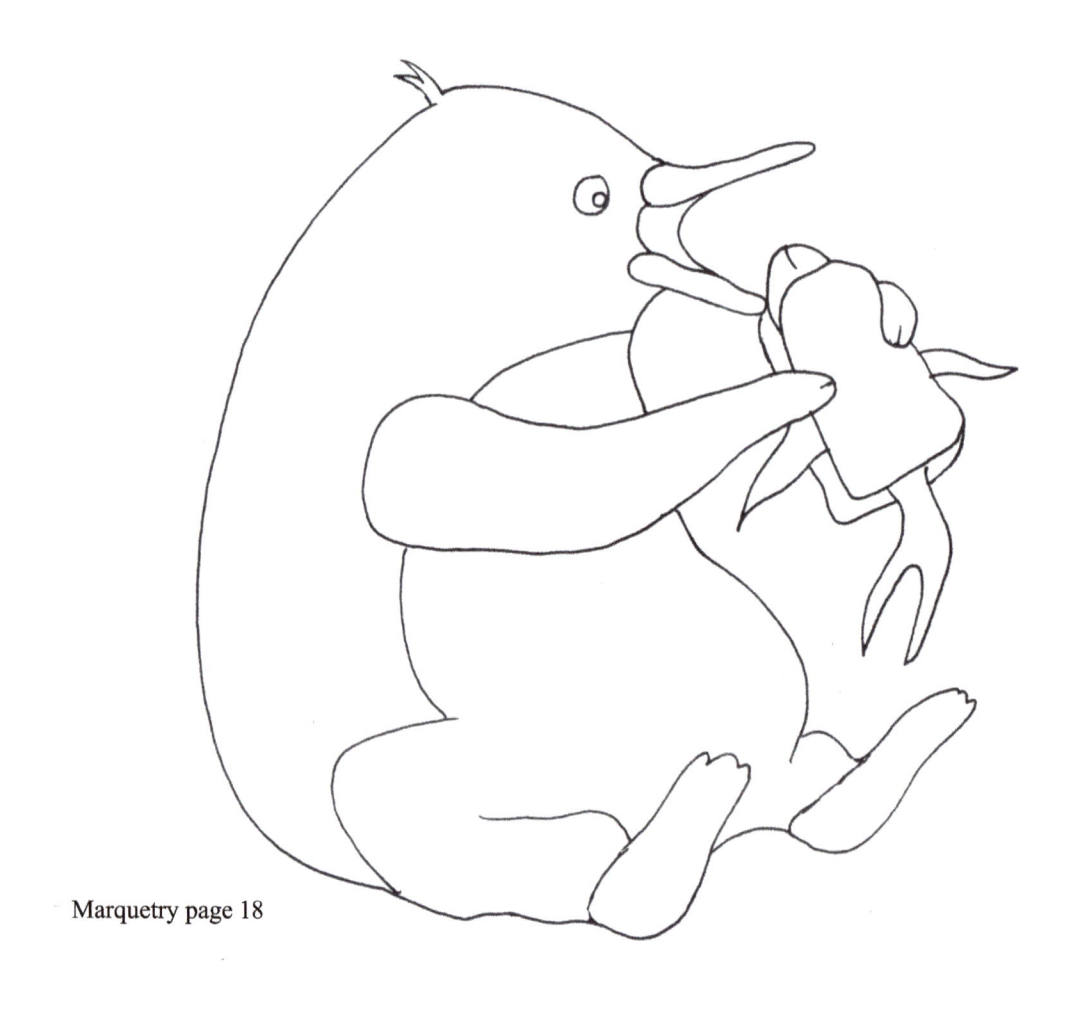

Marquetry page 18

Simple ornament, that, when retraced to obtain the symmetry, can ornate furniture.

Marquetry page 19

This drawing is s **"pricked"**.

Before the invention of the photocopier, to reproduce a drawing, artists placed it on many pieces of papers. He would prick the plan with a needle. He then rubbed each paper with a buffer of felt-tip coats of asphalt of Judea, a black powder that blackens the small holes. The he heated quickly the papers on a hot plate to fix the asphalt by melting it. (to prick he used a small hand held machine, of which the needle has the same movement as the sewing machine.

Marquetry details of the birds: page 29

7° RIM, année 2000

Les détails du tracé de ce "piqué" sont à interpréter relativement librement.

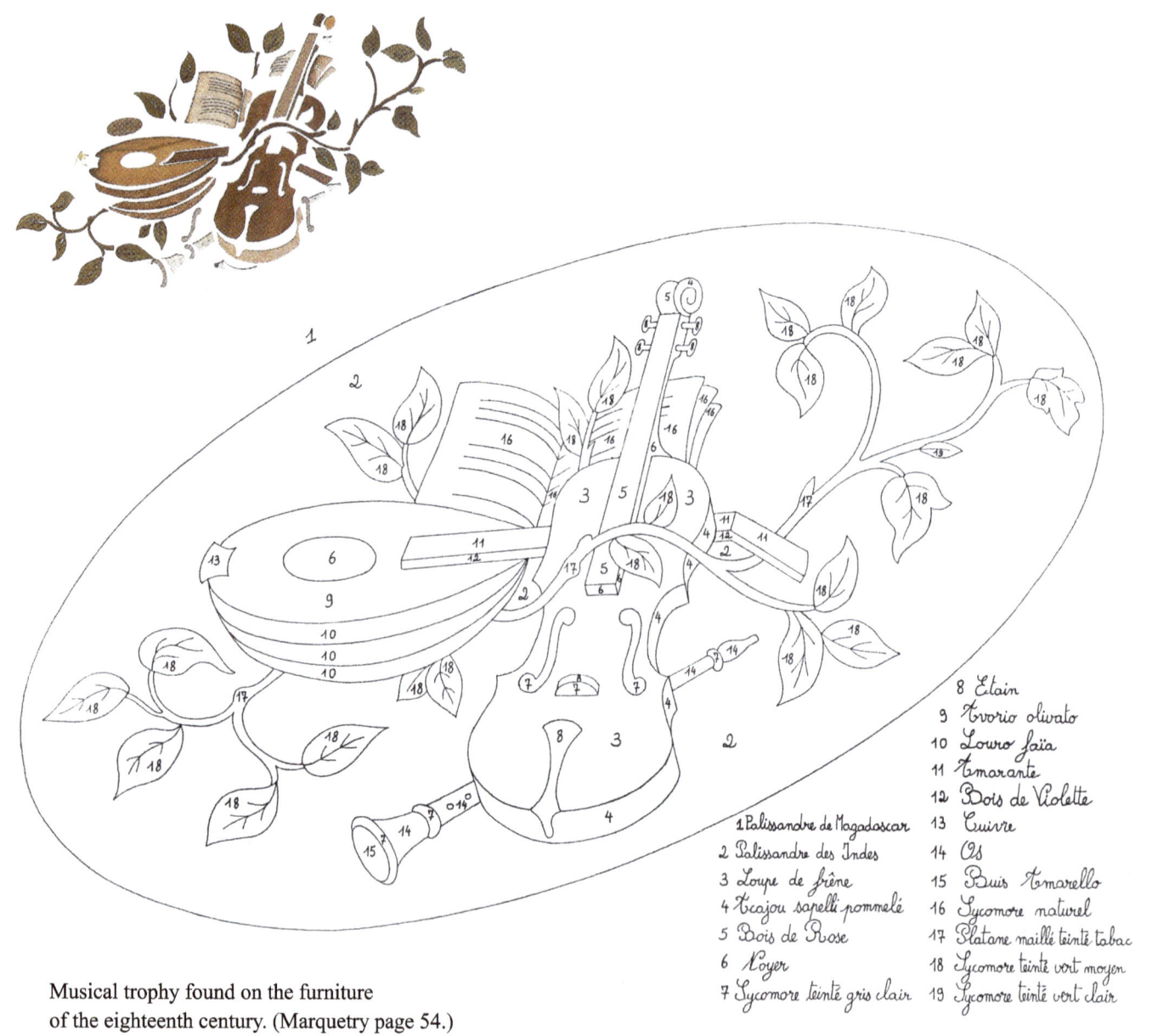

Musical trophy found on the furniture
of the eighteenth century. (Marquetry page 54.)

1. Rosewood from Madagascar 2. Indian rosewood 3. Magnifying glass ash tree
4. Mahogany dappled sapelli 5. Tulip wood 6. Walnut 7. Light gray tinted sycamore
8. Tin 9. Avorio olivato 10. Louro-faia 11. Amaranth 12. King wood 13. Copper
14. Bone 15. Amarello box tree 16. Natural sycamore 17. Meshed tinged plane tree tobacco
18. green tinted sycamore 19. light green tinted sycamore

Ornament on a chest

Légende des bois :
Fond en merisier
1 sycomore naturel
2 buis amarello
3 padouc ("bois de corail")
4 amarante
5 platane maillé teinté tabac
6 sycomore teinté vert foncé
   ou vert moyen
7 tulipier
8 poirier
9 noyer ou teck

Legend of the wood :

Wild cherry bottom
1 natural sycamore
2 amarello box tree
3 paddock
4 amaranth
5 meshed tinged plane tree tobacco
6 dark green tinted sycamore
7 tulip tree
8 pear tree
9 Walnut or teak

25 x 25 cm

Retraced drawing on a post stamp. Marquetry page 53.

Dog made by Philippe Guérin,

The valley of the elephants
42 x 30 cm
Wood choice
1. lemon tree
2. pink pear tree
3. mahogany dappled sapelli
4. rosewood from Madagascar
5. Indian rosewood
6. Light gray tinted sycamore
7. Dark gray tinted sycamore
8. Natural sycamore
9. Dark old green tinted sycamore
10. Amaranth
11. King wood
12. Walnut
13. Ash tree
14. Box tree
15. Louro-faia
16. Meshed tinged plane tree tobacco
17. Paddock
18. Magnifying glass of decorates tinged green
19. Sycamore light green colored wavy
20. Chestnut waves
21. Tulip wood
22. Bone (or ivory)
23. Tin (or aluminum)

The elephant eyes are made with water chestnut. Indicate the wood thread direction of the elements on one of the copies, by hatchings.

La vallée des éléphants
42 x 30 cm

Choix des bois (à titre indicatif).
1. Citronnier
2. Poirier rose
3. Acajou sapelli pommelé
4. Palissandre de Madagascar
5. Palissandre des Indes
6. Sycomore teinté gris clair
7. Sycomore teinté gris foncé
8. Sycomore naturel
9. Sycomore teinté vieux vert
10. Amarante
11. Bois de violette
12. Noyer
13. Frêne
14. Buis
15. Louro-faïa
16. Platane maillé teinté tabac
17. Padouk
18. Loupe d'orme teintée vert moyen
19. Sycomore ondé teinté vert clair
20. Marronnier ondé
21. Bois de rose
22. Os (ou ivoire…)
23. Etain (ou aluminium)
Les yeux des éléphants sont en nacre.

Indiquez le sens du fil des bois des éléments sur une des copies, par des hachures.

Temple of abundance.
35 x 20cm

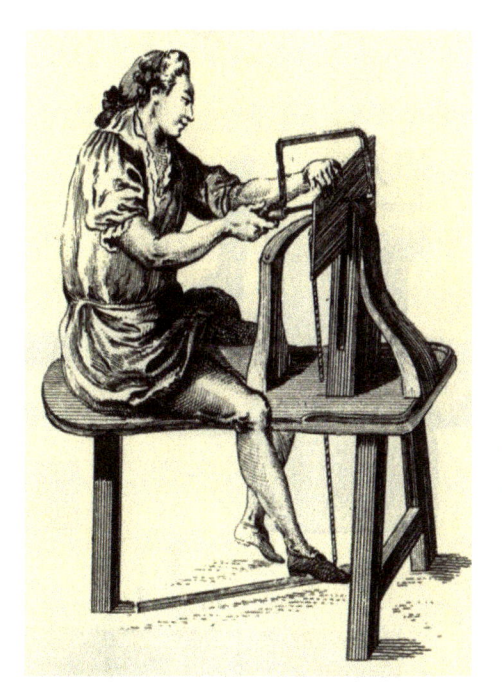

"Donkey" to trim an inlay in the eighteenth century.

Conclusion

Good work and my very best wishes for your happiness thanks to your new activity. Send me by email pictures of your works, I'll put some on my blog.

Thank you

My son Yann for his precious collaboration
Jean-Michel Marais for his beautiful drawings
Alexandre Nestora, photographer, for his wise advice

The second volume is an improvement: particular techniques, other materials other than wood, Boulle method, contemporary marquetry…

The third will speak of "frigates" : geometrical marquetry.

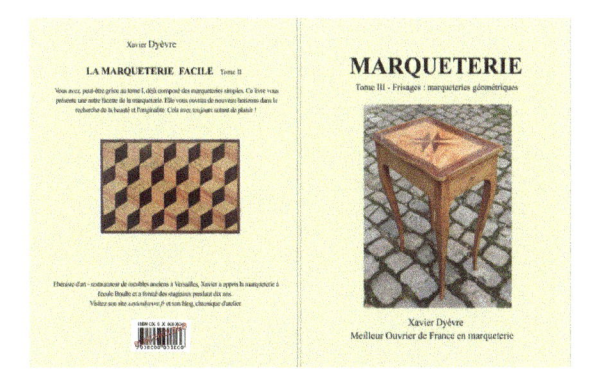

Marquetry Yann and Xavier Dyèvre, other than mentioned.   Pictures, lyout: Xavier. 2016
Mail: xavierdyevre@gmail.com - Chronicle of the workshop: www.blog.xavierdyevre.fr
Workshop of cabinetmaking : 15 rue du Peintre Lebrun 78000 Versailles

My marquetry of best worker of France in 1997: the windmill seen as a giant by a hallucinating Don Quixote. On the right, Sancho Panza on his donkey… bottom: bramble of ash tree. about forty woods or materials. About 900 hours. The subject was the drawing, but outlined rather fuzzy, in black and white. The candidates had one year to interpret freely at home. 85 x 65

Lightning Source UK Ltd.
Milton Keynes UK
UKHW021150290319
340053UK00001B/9/P